The Atlantic
Privateers

This old engraving shows a waterfront scene typical of the auction sales held to dispose of prize ships and cargoes.

The Atlantic Privateers

For my wife Nancy
semper fidelis

PREFACE

This book originated as part of Project Atlantic Canada (Atlantic Shore), one of the projects of the Canada Studies Foundation. Through this and other affiliated projects across the country CSF is attempting to foster the development of new curriculum, materials and teaching methods in the field of Canadian Studies. This study explores one aspect of a major theme of Project Atlantic Canada—The Relationships between the People and the Sea. This theme is one of a number of Continuing Canadian concerns to which CSF projects address themselves.

The purpose of CSF is not to produce a national text in Canadian Studies nor to encourage a single interpretation of these continuing concerns; the nature of Canadian Society renders such activity impossible. Rather, the objective is to draw to the attention of Canadians and especially Canadian students, issues which have been and continue to be of concern to the whole of our society in order that they might better understand the amalgam of diversity and unity that is the essence of Canadian society and gain a sense of belonging to a unique identifiable culture and the sharing of a rich heritage.

— The Canada Studies Foundation

Privateer brig "Rover", engaging a French squadron off the Atlantic Coast.

BOW SHOT

When I embarked on a study of shore communities for Canada Studies Foundation in the mid 70s, I little realized that it would result in the material on privateering. during the course of research I had occasion to inspect this phenomenon in its historical context and arrived at the conclusion that the whole business of privateering was of considerable consequence to Nova Scotia, New Brunswick, and, Newfoundland not only in military, but also in economic terms. What continues to be particularly evident is the ignorance that exists surrounding the activities of privateersmen and how the whole business was carried on. The net result when I first put pen to paper in 1978 was a determination to reveal briefly, the mechanics of this most fascinating matter. In 1999 my mission remains the same.

While several Atlantic ports harbored privateers, none was better known than Liverpool. One of the principle founders of Liverpool, Sylvanus Cobb, held a letter of marque for his sloop *York*. During the American Revolution, several Liverpool investors including Simeon Perkins, determined to carry the war to the rebels and outfitted the little sloop *Lucy* as a privateer. One of the investors was Captain John Howard whose company of the King's Orange Rangers had come to Liverpool in 1778 to help defend the community against rebel American privateers. Ironically, it was the capture of an American merchantman by the *Lucy* which led to the American raid on Fort Point in 1780 by Captain Cole and the brief internment of Captain Howard and most of his soldiers.

Around the turn of the 18 th century, the brig *Rover* was built at Herring Cove - modern Brooklyn - and cruised the Spanish Main capturing and bringing several

Spanish vessels back to Liverpool. On one cruise she defeated a Spanish fleet of four vessels inflicting tremendous damage to the enemy, but without loosing a single Nova Scotian. Later, in the war of 1812 the *Liverpool Packet* wrecked havoc on American shipping as far south as Nantucket. Liverpool was indeed the *Port of the Privateers*.

Suffice it to say that economic and military implications of privateering were of consequence. Privateers were to Atlantic Provinces what the militia was to Canada. They provided a means of defense managed at the local level and supplemented an economy whose trade patterns were disrupted by the many wars in which Britain found herself engaged during the eighteenth and early nineteenth centuries. Fortunes were made and lost and one man -Enos Collins of Liverpool and Halifax- became a multi-millionaire partly through his investments in privateering.

One can only hope that these few pages will help the reader to understand and appreciate this part of our Candian heritage better as well as prompt further interest in the phenomenon of privateering.

John G. Leefe
Liverpool, Nova Scotia
Port of the Privateers
May 1999

TABLE OF CONTENTS

ACTS OF HOSTILITY

Privateering is a very old profession whose origins are lost in the mists of time. When Europeans first came to America, they brought with them a custom of outfitting vessels of war which could legally sally forth in search of enemy shipping. It was because they operated under government licenses or letters-of-marque that privateers must be distinguished from pirates, buccaneers and other such free-booters.

The practice of letter-of-marque vessels operating in and out of Atlantic waters stretches back at least to 1613 when Samuel Argall captured and destroyed Poutrincourt's settlement at Port Royal. Later, during the French regime in Acadia, Port Royal (modern Annapolis Royal) became a centre for privateersmen operating against New England shipping. After the loss of Acadia to Britain in 1713 and the foundation of Louisbourg in 1726, the focal point of these rovers was changed to that fortress port.

It was not until the founding of Halifax in 1749 that Nova Scotian privateering began in earnest. Increasingly from this date on, Bluenoses, in times of war, traded their cargo manifests for letters-of-marque to seek fame and fortune on the high seas. The Seven Years' War, the American Revolution, the French Revolutionary and Napoleonic Wars and the War of 1812 saw thousands of seamen and hundreds of vessels embark on cruises designed to sting the enemy and enrich the privateersmen.

Newfoundland and New Brunswick, too, were active in the field. St. John's was a haven for English-owned vessels

1

preying on the trans-Atlantic traffic for which the colony served as a street corner in the trade between Europe and America. The city of Saint John, though late in developing its share of the trade, became an active privateering centre during the War of 1812. Only Prince Edward Island seems to have remained aloof from privateering although she did suffer from attacks by American vessels during the American Revolution.

Like any business enterprise, and indeed that is exactly what privateering was, a great deal of planning was necessary for every venture. The first qualification, of course, was that there had to be a war in progress and during the second half of the eighteenth century and early years of the nineteenth, this presented little problem. In the great quest for empire Britain, France, Spain and even the United States were frequently at each other's throats. Thus, if Britain was crossing swords with France—and it seems that this was generally the case—only British or French subjects could look forward to engaging in privateering.

Privateers Wharf — with kind permission of L. B. Jenson.

War always drove up insurance rates and frequently interrupted normal trading patterns, particularly in the West Indies where it seemed that just about every European nation controlled at least one island. Faced with these problems and with the prospect of gaining quick profits through the capture of enemy merchantmen, the merchants of Halifax, Saint John, Liverpool or St. John's often met in their homes, offices or a local tavern to discuss the possibility of outfitting a privateer. They would discuss what vessels were available, who might be a good choice as captain, where the vessel might go, what the costs would be and so on. Too, there was the added advantage on the part of these businessmen that through outfitting a privateer, they were striking a blow against the king's enemies. Once a voyage was decided upon, the merchants purchased shares in order to provide operating capital for the scheme.

Usually a privateering vessel was a converted merchantman although occasionally, as was the case with the *Rover* of Liverpool, she was built specifically for that purpose. There were dozens of designs available but the three most commonly employed in privateering were the sloop, schooner and brigantine. Often the locale in which the voyage was to take place would be a determining factor in the type of vessel chosen. This done, she was sent off to the nearest port which could supply guns, cutlasses, muskets, boarding pikes and all the other implements required for war and turned into a fighting vessel.

Upon return to the port she was to use as home base, the captain and his officers began recruiting a few using

4

some rather unique methods. Once a full complement was acquired, she was off on the briny blue in search of prey. Yet all these preparations were only the beginning of a relatively complex, sometimes rewarding and frequently dangerous adventure.

Despite the economic side of privateering, it should not be forgotten that it also provided a means of defence and offence managed at the local level, a weapon through which Nova Scotians, New Brunswickers and Newfoundlanders could do their bit for the empire of which they were part. The colony of Canada had her militia, so too did the older Atlanic colonies except that theirs was seabound and often fought thousands of miles from home. Indeed, it does not seem out of the way to suggest that in the privateers of these maritime provinces, lay the seeds of the Royal Canadian Navy.

THE SCHOONER PRIVATEER *LIVERPOOL PACKET*

Contrary to popular opinion, not all vessels are ships. There are sloops and schooners, brigs and brigantines, barques and barquentines and many, many others. Each style of rig and each hull design are suited to particular purposes. What type would best be suited to privateering? All sorts of factors would have to be considered. Where would most of her cruising take place? How many sailors would be needed to man her? Would she be deep or shallow in draught? How much hull space could reasonably be sacrificed for speed? Was she suited to carrying the heavy four and six pound cannons without losing seaworthingness? How much could the owners afford and what was available? All these factors and many more determined the kind of vessel which embarked on a privateering career.

On November 10, 1811, a sleek schooner, her two masts stepped at a rakish angle, slipped over the bar past Fort Point and the Widow Dexter's tavern and into Liverpool Harbour. She had sailed straight from Halifax where she had recently been condemned as a prize by the Court of Vice-Admiralty and auctioned in the rooms of the Spread Eagle at the Foot of Salter Street, selling for the great sum of £ 440. Built for speed in the carriage of an illegal cargo, this Baltimore clipper had dimensions which bespoke her trade— LOA 53 feet, beam 18 feet 11 inches, depth of hold 6 feet 6 inches, and weight 67 tons British admeasurement. She had been tender to a slaver, and was popularly named the *"Black Joke"*.

Among the bidders was a sharp Halifax merchant who had recently come to the capital from Liverpool, a bustling timber and fishing community some seventy miles down the coast. Being a man of shrewd reputation and some means, Enos Collins probably had little difficulty in outbidding his competitors who probably saw only limited usefulness in the foul smelling ex-slaver. After all, she was too narrow to accommodate general cargo on anything but a small scale, and she was certainly not suited to the fishery. So, on behalf of himself and his Liverpool partners, Benjamin Knaut and John and James Barss, he purchased the little vessel, had her fumigated with a concoction of vinegar, tar and brimstone and christened her *Liverpool Packet*.

**Captain Joseph Barss Jr. of the Privateer Schooner
Liverpool Packet**

Although war with the United States was several months away, Collins may have had a privateering career in mind for the *Liverpool Packet* when he purchased her. He was a keen business man, and seemed to possess a sixth sense which allowed him to make good decisions for future developments. Whether he had this foresight in this instance is not known, but when the War of 1812 was declared, the *Packet's* design obviously cut her out for a special role.

The *Liverpool Packet* was the most successful of all the privateers which ever sailed out of what are now Canadian ports. A large part of her good fortune may very well have been the result of her design. Deep in draught, she could sail close to the wind which gave her an advantage over many other designs. Coastal waters, though more dangerous for navigation, provided her with a rich crop of smaller, but less well defended vessels, and being simple in rig, she could be manned by a fairly small crew. Often only five or six sailors were left for the voyage home once her crew had been depleted in order to man the prizes she had captured. In addition, she could inconspicuously lie in wait shadowed against the black coastline. When a sail was sighted, she could crowd on canvas quickly, and run her down. She was large enough to carry a full crew of forty men and armament consisting of one six pounder and four twelves. Yet, she was small enough that upon two occasions, she was able to avoid capture by being rowed with great spruce oars, (part of the cargo of a captured vessel.) Finally, the speed made possible by her sharp design gave her the advantage of being quick in pursuit or in retreat.

During the War of 1812, the *Liverpool Packet* concentrated on raiding American shipping along the coast of New England and in the two years she served her owners, her prizes exceeded a quarter of a million dollars. Time and again she appeared like a wolf among sheep, frequently sailing right into the mouth of Boston harbour to make a capture. The New England newspapers reported her activities regularly.

THE *LIVERPOOL PACKET* HAS JUST CAPTURED AND SENT IN (TO LIVERPOOL) THE *DOLPHIN OF BEVERLY* WITH FLOUR AND TOBACCO; THE *COLUMBIA OF DENNIS* WITH 600 BARRELS OF FLOUR AND 203 KEGS OF TOBACCO; *TWO FRIENDS OF BOSTON,* WITH A CARGO OF FLOUR; AND THE *SUSAN OF SANDWICH,* WITH A CARGO OF FLOUR. SHE COULD HAVE CAPTURED MANY MORE, BUT HAD ONLY SEVEN MEN LEFT TO NAVIGATE HER TO LIVERPOOL.

The greatest testimony to the success of the *Liverpool Packet* was written on New Year's Day 1813 in the Boston *Messenger:*

THE DEPREDATIONS REPEATEDLY COMMITTED ON OUR COASTING TRADE BY THIS PRIVATEER SEEM TO BE NO LONGER REGARDED THE MOMENT WE HEAR SHE HAS LEFT OUR BAY (MASSACHUSETTS BAY) FOR THE PURPOSE OF CONVOYING PRIZES SAFELY INTO PORT, ALTHOUGH THE PROPERTY TAKEN BE ENORMOUS. THAT AN INSIGNIFICANT FISHING SCHOONER OF FIVE AND THIRTY TONS (sic)

SHOULD BE SUFFERED TO APPROACH THE HARBOUR OF THE METROPOLIS OF MASSACHUSETTS, CAPTURE AND CARRY HOME IN TRIUMPH EIGHT OR NINE VESSELS OF SAIL VALUED AT FROM SEVENTY TO NINETY THOUSAND DOLLARS, AND OWNED ALMOST EXCLUSIVELY BY MERCHANTS IN BOSTON, IN THE SHORT SPACE OF TWENTY DAYS FROM THE TIME SHE LEFT LIVERPOOL, N.S., WOULD SEEM UTTERLY INCREDIBLE WERE THE FACT NOT PLACED BEYOND ANY DOUBT. LET IT BE REMEMBERED TOO, THAT THE SEVENTY OR NINETY THOUSAND DOLLARS ARE THE FRUITS OF BUT ONE CRUISE, AND THAT THIS SAME MARAUDER HAD BUT A FEW WEEKS BEFORE CAPTURED WITHIN TEN MILES OF CAPE COD, VESSELS WHOSE CARGOES WERE WORTH AT LEAST FIFTY THOUSAND DOLLARS.

While her size and speed allowed her to run in and out of American waters almost at will, it also prevented her from being captured on two occasions in April 1813. While cruising off Cape Cod she had the misfortune to fall in with the larger American privateer *New Orleans* commanded by Captain John Crocker. Fortunately, the Bluenosers had only a few days before captured the *Defiance* and had taken aboard several long sweeps or huge oars which had been in the enemy cargo. While light winds prevented the *New Orleans* from overtaking her, the *Packet's* crew manned the sweeps and rowed their sixty-five ton schooner to freedom. Only a few days later she re-enacted the same drama, this time in the vicinity of Martha's Vineyard. Lying in Tarpaulin Cove on Naushon Island, she was discovered by the Falmouth privateer *Little Duck* but once again relying on the sweeps of the *Defiance* she was able to escape.

However, if size was an advantage, it could also be a disadvantage. This Captain Joseph Barss and his Nova Scotian crew found out on June 11, 1812. On that day the American privateer *Thomas* sailed into Portsmouth, New Hampshire towing a captured schooner. Captain Shaw could well be pleased with himself for his prize was none other than the *Liverpool Packet*. The crew of the *Packet* were hurriedly put ashore, and turned over to the United States Marshal. Guarded by militiamen, they were marched along Islington Street to the tune of jeers from the large crowd which had quickly assembled and cast into jail. Captain Barss was given a particularly difficult time, for he was locked in fetters, and fed on a diet of water and hard tack. The hatred of the New Englanders for this too successful enemy was expressed by William Damerell, the *Thomas's* Second Lieutenant when he remarked on his "great sorrow he had not put every soul on the *Liverpool Packet* to death."

The *Liverpool Packet* was subsequently sold to a Captain Watson who took her on a cruise under her new flag. He in turn sold her to William B. Dobson who had formerly been skipper of the American privateer *Young Teazer* which had blown up in Mahone Bay some months before. After one cruise with no prizes, he in turn sold her to Captain John Perkins who renamed her the *Portsmouth Packet*. During her first cruise under Perkins she was captured by H.M.S. *Fan-*

tome off Mount Desert Island after a thirteen hour chase. On November 9, 1813 she was sold as a prize at Halifax to the firm of Collins and Allison and returned to her home port of Liverpool under her old name. Placed under the command of Captain Caleb Seely of Saint John and later Lewis Knaut of Liverpool, she continued to work successfully as a privateer until December 1814 when she captured her last prize.

Once a privateering cruise had been decided upon, it was necessary for the owners and captain to receive a licence or letter-of-marque from the governor. If a vessel operated without such a document, the captain and his crew would be considered pirates, and the penalty for piracy was hanging. Sometimes the owner happened to be the captain, and if he could not afford a letter-of-marque, he would arrange to borrow the bond money, usually by promising shares in any prizes he might capture. This was the case with Silvanus Cobb, a native of Plymouth, Massachusetts, who, from 1745 to his death in 1761, spent much of his life cruising in Nova Scotia water.

Halifax 20th Novemr 1757

Letter of Marque to Silvanus Cobb Commander of the Sloop York & Halifax ————

The Sloop York and Halifax; burthen about Eighty Tons Silvanus Cobb Commander carrying about Forty Men Daniel Wise Lieu. Serjeant Jeremiah House Master and Isaac West Boatswain, Victualled for Cruizing on the Coast of Nova Scotia to protect the Trade carrying Six Carriage and four Swivle Guns with Furniture and Ammunition in pro = portion

signed

The same Day a Bail Bond given according to the foregoing in the Sum of Fifteen hundred Pounds Sterling by Charles Procter Esqr. and Joseph Gray Merchant.

And thereupon was Issued a Letter of Marque under the Governors hand and Seal to Captain Cobb to the said Sloop York and Halifax according to the Tenor of the Commission before inserted. ——

Letter of Marque.

Letter-of-Marque to Silvanus Cobb Commander of the Sloop York and Halifax:

Halifax, 20 November 1757

The Sloop York and Halifax, burthen about Eighty Tons Silvanus Cobb Commander carrying about Forty Men Daniel Wise Lieutenant Jeremiah House Master and Isaac West Boatswain, victualled for Cruizing on the Coast of Nova Scotia to protect the Trade Carrying Six Carriage and four Swivle Guns with Furniture and Ammunition in proportion.

Signed

The same Day a Bail Bond given according to the foregoing in the Sum of Fifteen hundred Pounds Sterling by Charles Procter, Esq. and Joseph Gray Merchant.
And thereupon was Issued a Letter of Marque under the Governors hand and Seal to Captain Cobb to the said Sloop York and Halifax according to the Tenor of the Commission before inserted.

With the assurance that he could legally attack enemy shipping, the captain now had to get his vessel ready for the voyage. Cobb's sloop was already armed, but many, when they received their letters-of-marque, were not. This meant a trip to His Majesty's Dockyard in Halifax, where various types of cannons—four, six, eight, or twelve pounders, or the smaller swivels—would be shipped along with powder, shot, cordage and blocks for tackle, ramrods, swabs and wadding. This done, all the stores for the voyage would be stowed below—extra cordage for rigging, canvas for repairs to sails, extra suits of sails, spare anchors, anchor cables, barrels of water and salt pork, and of course, kegs of rum. Cutlasses, pistols, muskets and sometimes pikes were brought on board as well as grappling irons and boarding nets. Every necessity was acquired and stowed so the vessel would not be caught short.

RENDEZ-VOUS AND RIOT

Thursday, May 11, 1780, the fifth year of war in America, a fresh spring rain fell on Liverpool and spattered gently against the bull's eye window panes of Simeon Perkins' counting room. Four men sat about the room, comfortably situated in the painted Windsor chairs and warmed by talk of business and the minor successes of the town's first privateer, the *Lucy*. Perkins, Joe Tinkham and Will Freeman were prominent merchants in the township as well as leading figures in its public life. They had another thing in common too, for they were the owners of the *Lucy* and were planning her next cruise against the rebels. With them sat thirty-five year old Captain Joe Freeman, fisherman, shipmaster and trader to the southern colonies and the West Indies. Being Nova Scotian Yankees, it did not take long to come to the business at hand for the *Lucy's* owners were determined to have Freeman serve as master of their vessel during the cruise they were busy planning. They accordingly offered him the lieutenant's berth and "Some Other prerequisits for Inducements". Captain Freeman listened attentively, suggested that he would prefer to consider their offer and left to go about his daily business. The owners had not long to wait for the next morning he agreed to accept their offer providing a £10 bonus was given him.

Monday morning found Joe Freeman stepping lightly along the street in the spring sunshine. His destination was Mrs. West's tavern and a "rendez-vous" or recruiting party to begin the task of filling out the *Lucy's* crew. Entering the good widow's establishment, he seated himself at a table with pen and paper ready to sign on hands. The town's taverns were always bustling with sailors from several of the colonies and West's was one of the most popular. By day's end fourteen men, including officers had entered, a good start but hardly enough to warrant too great enthusiasm. Thus the rendez-vous continued through the next day with the added factor of Stephen Smith departing from Lunenburg and La-Have to seek more recruits.

As if there was not enough competition in seeking hands, Ben Collins arrived at Mrs. West's on the 18th to establish a rendez-vous for Captain Tom Ross's privateer brig *Resolution*. Ross, a native of Falmouth, Massachusetts, had come to Liverpool as a Loyalist refugee where he remained until 1785 when he moved to Grand Manan in the spanking new colony of New Brunswick. Collins, too, was pressed to fill out his crew for he had worked his way down the coast through Halifax and Lunenburg. Such competition could lead to rather varying circumstances.

Not to be outdone, Will Freeman gathered his recruits together at West's, likely fortified them with a goodly portion of the owner's West Indian rum and "Dress'd with Ribands", paraded them through the streets of Liverpool. Whatever impression these antics may have had, both men signed on an equal number of hands throughout the day. Meanwhile, Captain Ross's shallop was spirited away from its place at Simeon Perkins' wharf and a small anchor and a quantity of pork removed. Possibly some of *Lucy's* men had decided to deal with the competition on their own terms. The *Lucy's* owners would have none of this, however, and immediately offered to make good the loss. Nonetheless, Perkins recorded in his diary that "Some Disputes have happened between recruiting parties."

May 20th brought rain and it also brought trouble. The opposing crews grew larger, many of them spending their time milling about Mrs. West's drinking and discussing the virtues of their chosen vessels. Unfortunately, the discussion began to get out of hand and turned into fullscale argument until finally it became a "Quarrel arising to a great height," as Perkins put it. Ben Collins and Joe Tinkham did their best to calm the situation but with little luck, so sent a message to Fort Point to bring soldiers to control the privateersmen before they turned to full scale riot.

John Cameron hurried off to inform Lt. McLeod that the services of the King's Orange Rangers were required rather hastily. On the way to the fort he stopped at Perkin's house to inform him of the situation. Simeon, who was also a magistrate, rushed off to West's in company with Cameron but when they arrived they found "all matters were settled."

Cooler heads prevailed over the next few days and recruiting continued without incident. Peter Leonard promised to go in the *Lucy* for "1 barrel flower, 4 Gallons Molasses, 14 lbs. Sugar and 2 shirts" and a promise from Perkins that should Leonard be lost, his family would not suffer. Prince Snow returned on May 24 with three Lunenburgers, George Fiedel, James Crooks and Philip Arenburg with a promise of three more recruits to follow the next Sunday. A further problem arose when John Reynolds, the *Lucy's* master asked to be relieved of his post due to personal problems. Fortunately, John Mullins offered to take his place for £5 and supplies for his family.

With no more recruits to be had in Liverpool, the *Lucy* sailed for Barrington on June 8th to fill out her crew. Here she found men from Argyle and Yarmouth who were seeking a privateersman's berth and completed her task. She cruised the Gulf of Maine for three weeks, sending in six prizes, five empty schooners "of small value" and a brig loaded with salt.

If the *Lucy's* cruise was disappointing, Ross's venture in the *Resolution* was downright disasterous. On July 13th, Perkins recorded in his diary that off Halifax the *Resolution:*

had a Severe engagement Near the Light House (Sambro) with the Ship *Viper,* Captain Williams, from Boston for 3 Glasses. Capt. Ross lost 8 or 9 men, and his vessel much Disabled. He was obliged to Strike . . .

Among the killed is Mr. Raphael Wheeler & Silas Harlow of this Town & John Caldwell of this Neighbourhood.

Such were the rewards of privateering to some.

CHAMPAGNE AND SHIP'S BISCUIT

Like her sister province of New Brunswick, Newfoundland too was late entering into the business of privateering. That is not to say that prize auctions were anything out of the ordinary in St. John's. During the American Revolution dozens of Yankee vessels sailed under the brow of Signal Hill manned by Royal Navy prize crews. It was during the War of 1812, however, that Newfoundlanders sailed in privateers such as the *Fly* and *Star* so that by war's end over thirty American prizes had been brought into St. John's Harbour. When special trading licences for New England-Newfoundland trade were issued by the governor in 1815, eleven of the seventeen vessels receiving them were actually American in origin. Judge William Carter, who presided over the Court of Vice-Admiralty, must have been very busy indeed.

The cargo of one American prize consisted entirely of champagne and was carefully stored in the warehouses of Hunt, Stabb, Preston & Company. As a Sunday pastime three of the firm's employees, Ewen Stabb, Sam Prowse and Tom Brooking, took to placing champagne bottles on a gumphead at the end of the wharf. They then coolly took aim with their pistols and did their best to blow the heads off the bottles. The winner received a case of the bubbly stuff while the loser paid for it. While Ewen and his friends might wile away a pleasant afternoon playing over a privateer's booty, there had to be men to win it in the first place.

British brig "Observer" takes the American privateer "Jack" off Halifax, May 1782.

As enchanting as privateering may seem, with swash-buckling tars, sea duels and notions of quick wealth, it was mostly hard work with brief moments of fun and comradeship. A sailing vessel was a demanding servant, the sea a hard taskmaster. Scrambling aloft in a blow with the sea lashed into frothing fury demanded courage and the agility of a cat. Shortening sail 90 feet above a pitching deck in the total darkness of night required the dexterity of the angels themselves. Your feet became your lifeline, clutching desperately at the footropes as your hands grappled with chafing canvas, the wind lashing your back—a friend pressing you against the yard rather than dashing you to pulp on the deck below. Still, you considered yourself fortunate not to be on deck where the waves could pluck you up, and fling you into the sea, or deep in the ship breaking your back pumping out the sea-water which had flowed in through sprung planks.

Napoleon once remarked that an army marched on its stomach. This may have been the case with the army, but it certainly was not for a sailor. With the likelihood of being out of sight of land or sailing in enemy territory where going ashore was just too risky, it was necessary to ship food which had one quality—it would spoil slowly. With this in mind, great quantities of ship's biscuits in large wooden casks were stored in the hold. To say the least, they did provide an appetizing diet. One poor soul described them as being "so hard that we often used the cannon balls to break it even into pieces" and there were "so many worms that we just had to eat them too, as a butter substitute." Salted beef and pork hardened to the consistency of shoe leather, so hard in fact that sailors often carved it into decorative geegaws. As if this were not enough, the water, fresh when brought abroad, became foul with "thick finger-long fibres in it giving it a glutinous consistency." Lack of fresh fruit weakened the body so that scurvy loosened the teeth till they could be pulled out with your fingers, and swelled your limbs till the pain either killed you or made you wish it would. The cramped quarters with hammocks slung between decks were breeding grounds for disease. With no ventilation, the air stagnated, you froze in the high latitudes, and baked in low.

A sailor's day was divided into six periods or "watches", the number of watches he worked depending on the size of the crew. Still, it should not be assumed that when he had stood his watches, his work for the day was done. During a storm or when a strange sail hove in sight the boatswains rapped on the hatch covers calling all hands on deck. Tumbling out of their hammocks, the tired sailors had to be prepared for even the most tiring tasks at a moment's notice. Even in port there was work to be done, especially keeping the vessel fit.

Occasionally a vessel had to be extensively overhauled far from home. This was especially true if she had spent some time in tropical waters where bottoms fouled much more quickly. Not to clean a hull could be an invitation to disaster for a dirty bottom made the vessel sluggish even under a full spread of canvas.

Every minute spent in refit was a minute lost for cruising against the enemy with the result that a twelve hour day was common fare. The vessel had to be emptied and the goods and guns put on shore right down to the ballast. The empty hold could then be scrubbed clean of filth which had accumulated during the voyage. The yards were removed from the masts to prevent them from putting too great a strain on the rigging or damaging the masts themselves.

This done, the vessel was taken into shore at high tide so that when the tide ran out, the vessel would roll gently on her side. Now the sailors could busily scrape the hull while carpenters wittled plugs to fill holes made by torpedo worms. When the tide rose she righted herself only to roll to her other side when it fell again. Thus the opposite side could be cleaned. When the hull was cleared of the algae and barnacles and the holes plugged, a "good Coat of Hot Stuff was applied to discourage further fouling."

Meanwhile the rigging was checked, railings repaired or rebuilt, sails sewn and so on. Once this was all completed, the whole process was reversed until the vessel was ready for sea once more. It was not unusual for this procedure to take as much as two weeks of backbreaking labour under a scorching southern sun.

Yet, despite the evils, you were drawn back to sea again and again for it was not a way of life, but life itself. Living and working together, often in the face of peril, made men dependent on each other, and created a special comradeship that was comfortable in times of ease, essential in times of crisis. Almost always there was a shipmate who could scrape out a tune on a fiddle or squeeze a song out on an accordian. There were the good times like Christmas at sea with singing, dancing of jigs and an extra tot all around. There were the rituals too, like the visit of King Neptune to those who were crossing the line for the first time. And there were the still moments as the captain raised his voice in prayer, and a shipmate, wrapped in canvas with a cannonball at this feet, slid from beneath his country's flag to be committed to eternal rest in the soul of the deep.

It was not a life for idle men, the boatswain knew how to deal with them. A happy ship was a good ship, and a good ship was one in which every sailor knew his task and his place. They lived hard, and they gained a reputation for their activities on shore which has been handed on to the sailors of today. This is truly the age of wooden ships and iron men.

BEAT TO QUARTERS

The spring of 1800 found Britain at war with Spain and republican France. In Liverpool, Nova Scotia, Snow Parker had acquired the services of Captain Alexander Godfrey as commander of the newly built brig *Rover,* a 100 ton vessel built especially with privateering in mind. With the *Rover* nearly ready for sea, Alex Godfrey sailed for Halifax in order to apply for a letter-of-marque and take on various pieces of armament at His Majesty's Dockyard including fourteen four-pound cannons.

Cover painting for Thomas H. Raddall's novel, Prides
Fancy, a story of a Nova Scotian privateer in the Wars
of the French Revolution. Painting presently in the col-
lection of John Leefe.

With a crew of 55 men and boys, the *Rover* cruised southward and on June 17 fell in with a French convoy of six vessels to the westward of Puerto Rico. Despite the fact that one of the enemy vessels carried sixteen guns and another six, the convoy scattered rather than attack. By nightfall the *Rover* had won the American whaler *Rebecca* carrying a valuable cargo of 1100 barrels of spermaceti oil and American brig *Moses Myers,* deeply laden with a cargo of wine. These two vessels had been prizes to a French privateer despite the fact that France and the United States were technically at peace. That was no concern of Alex Godfrey, however, for he had won them quite legally. On July 4, 1800, exactly a month after leaving Liverpool, Godfrey returned home with these two valuable prizes as well as a third captured on the homeward voyage.

Two weeks later the *Rover* departed on another cruise, this time deep in Carribean waters. Meeting with no luck on the high seas, Godfrey set his sights on the coasting traders of the Spanish Main, that great stretch of coast which today forms the shore of Venezuela. Here the strategy was to send a cutter under command of Lodowick Harrington, the *Rover's* mate, to seize small vessels under cover of darkness. While not a very exciting pastime, it did provide a great quantity of cocoa for the *Rover's* hold. This type of operation proved so successful that Godfrey sent Harrington and the cutter crew on a longer voyage with the intention of meeting a few days later but this was not to be.

The Spanish authorities at Puerto Cabello had not been idle and were busy laying a trap for this testy brig which was disrupting their coastal trade. Carefully they spun their web, using a large trading schooner as bait. Early on the morning of September 10, a light breeze wafted the Spanish schooner out of Puerto Cabello and into the arms of the *Rover*. Godfrey immediately pursued her, chasing her towards the land where she drove herself aground. Too late did the Liverpool captain realize that he had sprung the Spanish trap. To make matters worse the breeze had dropped and the *Rover* lay becalmed.

Out of Puerto Cabello came a large schooner, the *Santa Rita,* armed to the gunwales with ten six pounders, two twelve pound cannonades, one hundred sailors and twenty-five marines. Lack of wind proved no problem to the Spaniards for the schooner was towed by two large galleys each carrying a six pounder in the bow, thirty marines and rowed by a mass of sweating black slaves chained to their oars. In addition a third galley pulled beside them in an effort to cut the *Rover* off from the open sea. The odds against the Nova Scotian seemed overwhelming. In anticipation of the worst, Alex Godfrey sent his nephew Henry to the powder magazine with orders to fire the ship if taken by the Spaniards.

A light breeze wafted down from the mountains which allowed the *Rover* to at least claw further away from the shore. At the same time the *Santa Rita* dropped her towlines and made for the privateer, intending to board. Godfrey used the one card he held. Ordering twenty-four of his forty-five men to port, they thrust great sweeps into the sea and spun the *Rover* around to bring her broadside to bear on the crowded schooner. Caught unaware, the *Santa Rita* was smashed by the *Rover's* four pounders. Without waiting to assess the damage they had inflicted, the Nova Scotians rushed to starboard, thrust their oars into the Carribean and spun around to face the two closest galleys, firing three guns into the first and four into the second.

Despite the shock of the *Rover's* attack, the *Santa Rita* fought bravely back while the two mauled galleys retreated momentarily to lick their wounds. Dead and seriously wounded alike were cast overboard much to the satisfaction of a growing number of sharks. The two larger vessels traded several broadsides, unaware of the damage they were able to inflict until the wind came up and blew the great hanging clouds of smoke away. Now was the *Rover's* chance to make her escape.

Just as she began to pull up for the open sea, a loud crack was heard from the *Santa Rita* as her foretopmast fell in a great heap across her bow. With rigging, sails and mast dragging in the water she was momentarily out of control. Quickly Godfrey drove the *Rover* to the Spaniard's side and grappling, ordered boarders away. In a few minutes it was all over, the Spanish colours fluttered to the blood strewn deck and the galleys ran for the protection of Puerto Cabello. Fifty-four Spaniards, including all but one young officer, were dead. Amazingly not one of the *Rover's* crew had been hurt.

On October 16, 1800 the *Rover* sailed into Liverpool Bay accompanied by the *Santa Rita,* her hard won prize. Simeon Perkins recorded the event that evening as he penned the daily entry in his diary.

32

Early this morning the brig *Rover*, Alexander Godfrey commander, arrived with an armed Spanish schooner ... which after a severe engagement the *Rover* took ... on the Spanish Main ... Mr. Lodowick Harrington was absent with ten more men, so that the *Rover* had only 38 men on deck in this engagement. We must esteem it a wonderful Interposition of Divine Providence. O! That men would praise the Lord for His Goodness and for His wonderful works to the Children of men.

Five days later Lud Harrington sailed into Liverpool on his prize, the *Nuestra Senora del Carmen*. After near starvation, he had brought her safely home making only one stop at Cape Cod to secure a little food, a voyage of 2,000 miles. On November 22 she was auctioned off at Liverpool for £238 while the *Santa Rita* was sent to Halifax where she was sold for £840. Who purchased them? None other than one Alexander Godfrey.

COURT OF VICE-ADMIRALTY

While many privateers had little success, others found Lady Luck more obliging. On one cruise the *Liverpool Packet* made her first capture on October 17, 1812, and her nineteenth on November 18. In three months, March to May 1813, the brig *Sir John Sherbrooke* captured no less than seventeen prizes. The sloop *Dart* sailing out of Saint John under Captain John Harris captured eleven vessels between July and September 1, 1813. She seems to have concentrated her efforts along the coast of Maine from Machias to Portland.

Privateering being legal, it was necessary to have laws to govern its practice. In order to ensure that each captured vessel was truly a prize of war, each would have its case heard before the judge of the Court of Vice-Admiralty in Halifax. The decisions did not always favour the captors, for sometimes the vessel would be declared not to have been an enemy. In some cases, the vessel might be declared forfeit while its cargo was released. In order for a vessel or its cargo to be proclaimed a prize of war, it had to be proven beyond a reasonable doubt that it was owned by a citizen of a hostile nation.

Once the Court had established that a capture was legal, the prize could be auctioned to the highest bidder. However, not all the profit from the sale went to the privateer which had captured her. There were court costs, governor's fees, crown fees, marshal's fees, storage, wharfage, and auction costs.

On April 16, 1755, Silvanus Cobb, cruising in the East Passage, detained the schooner *Wolfe*. Finding that the vessel was smuggling, and not on a fishing voyage as her master, William Clark, protested, he brought her into Halifax. The case was brought before the Court of Vice-Admiralty on April 18. Judge Collier declared that the schooner "with all her tackle, apparels, and furniture is to be sold at public auction on Wednesday at 10 of the clock in the Forenoon at Malachi Salter's storehouse." The value of the prize was set at £70.7.10 but Cobb received far less than that amount.

THE SETTLEMENT

Amount of Sale	£70.7.10	
Marshal's Commission to Prize Court	1.8. 1	68.19.9
Charges to be deducted		
Condemnation Fees	3.10.4	
Poundage	3. 9	
Warrant of Appraisement	.19	
3 Appraisers, 1 day each	1.10	
Malachi Salter for Wharfage Storage	1.15	
Marshall's Bill for Custody of the		
Vessel landing and measuring	5.13	
Silvanus Cobb for Pilotage	2.	
Advocates Fees	1.10	20. 6.4
		48.13.5
Distribution		
To His Majesty ⅓	16.4.6	
To His Excellency the		
Commander in Chief ⅓	16.4.6	
To Sylvanus Cobb, the		
Informer ⅓	16.4.6	

This was not the end of the division for Cobb's share had next to be divided amongst the crew. Privateering does not seem to have been quite so lucrative as popular history suggests.

REASON TO BE THANKFUL

On May 4, 1762, a Connecticut schooner warped over the river bar and made its way into the mouth of the Mersey River. Simeon Perkins stood in the vessel's waist. Leaning thoughtfully on the much worn railing, his enquiring glance fell upon the fish flakes which crowded down to the waters edge and on to little Knowle's Island which lay above the mouth of Liverpool Harbour. Gliding past Dean's Point and following the channel inside the island, the site of the township's heart came into view. Only two years old, Liverpool stretched from the Mill Brook upstream to Silvanus Cobb's handsome gambrel roofed house. Clinging to the shore with the brooding forest behind, it provided a panorama of straggling wharves, fish sheds and warehouses and behind them, a few streets deep, a growing town of small houses and huts. So this was to be Simeon's new home.

A merchant by trade and a native of Norwich, Connecticut, he and his partners Jabez Perkins and Ebenzer Backus had determined upon testing the industry of this little bit of New England transplanted in the rugged soil of Nova Scotia's South Shore. Within the day of his arrival he rented a store and watched over the unloading of the trade goods he had brought to stock it. Little could he have realized on that early May day that he would spend almost all of the next fifty years in this town and play a major part in its successes and failures as it struggled from infancy towards a vibrant maturity.

A business man always, he maintained his store until his death in November 1812. From this meagre beginning he went on to build vessels in Liverpool, nearby Herring Cove and Port Medway. Frequently his keen eye caught sight of a well found vessel under construction or lying at anchor in the harbour and he purchased a part interest in it. His little empire expanded through the years and he built a sawmill at the Falls to provide lumber to accompany the fish he exported from Liverpool.

His vessels which ranged in size from tiny sloops to full rigged ships, were to be found on the Grand Banks, along the coast of Labrador and on the banks of Nova Scotia eagerly seeking fish. As well, they were to be found plying the coastal trade of New England and sailing to the West Indies as far south as Venezuela and the fabled Spanish Main. Even the stormy North Atlantic proved no barrier for he also sent cargoes to Europe itself.

As a person he was forthright and honest and not a little bit affected by religion. Like most New Englanders who came to Nova Scotia, including that part which is now New Brunswick, he was a Congregationalist. While he played a prominent role in the Church's affairs, he was later impressed by the evangelical fervour of the New Lights and ended his life as a Methodist. His diary, which spans some forty-five years of his life in Liverpool, shows him to have been a man of deep religious conviction.

Never a person to shirk from public duty, he at one time or other, held every major appointment his community had to offer. He did not always seek these positions and more often than not accepted them because he felt it his duty as a citizen. Generally, these appointments fell into four categories: local government, provincial government, the military and justice. In the first he served as proprietor's clerk for Liverpool Township, town clerk, and county treasurer for Queens. In the second, he served several terms as the Member of the Legislative Assembly, sometimes representing Liverpool, other times representing Queens County. In the third instance, he served as deputy commissary of the troops stationed in Liverpool during the American Revolution and Lieutenant-Colonel of the Queens County Militia. In order to ensure the presence of justice in the community, he acted as Justice of the Peace, Judge of Probates, Deputy Registrar of the Court of Vice-Admiralty, and for forty-six years served as Judge of the Inferior Court of Common Pleas. It seems an understatement to say that he was a very public-spirited man.

That Perkins and the other principal merchants of his time were frequently involved in investing in privateering gives every reason to believe that it was considered an honest, even honourable pastime. In 1779 Perkins, Joseph Tinkham and William Freeman purchased the sloop *Lucy* and at a cost of £2,000 outfitted her to try to repay some of the damage done Liverpool vessels by American privateers. Despite the fact that this little Nova Scotian privateer captured six vessels including a sloop with a cargo valued at £2,241, he lost £35 in the venture. In addition, he and his partners lost every penny they had invested in a second privateer, the *Delight*, when she was taken from her wharf by the American privateerman Captain Ben Cole. Still, they were more fortunate than the owners of the privateer *Dispatch*. That cruiser captured the brig *Diana*, the owners were sued and lost £7,800 before they got out of court. Investing in three other privat-

39

eers during the Revolution, he never even made enough to cover his initial investment.

Despite this rather rocky start, Perkins and his fellow merchants eagerly invested in privateers when Britain went to war with revolutionary France in 1798. An even bigger bonus for Nova Scotians was the fact that a state of war also existed with Spain and the Batavian Republic as they had joined France. It was quite clear to them that their knowledge of the Carribean and the numerous enemy territories there could provide rich pickings.

Duke of Kent

Charles Mary Wentworth

Earl Spencer

In 1798 Perkins and several associates, including Snow Parker, his next door neighbour, built a 130 ton full rigged ship especially designed as a privateer. Wisely naming her after Governor Wentworth's son, Charles Mary Wentworth, the owners were able to enlist his support in acquiring sixteen guns valued at some £50 each. It was simply a matter of sailing to His Majesty's Dockyard at Halifax to pick them up. In addition, Perkins was able to persuade his friend Richard John Uniacke, the province's attorney-general, to convince Admiral Vandeput to provide shot and powder at government expense.

On August 15, 1798, the *Charles Mary Wentworth* commenced the first of three cruises, leaving Liverpool with a crew of sixty-seven men and boys. By the time she was sold in 1800 she had captured in excess of ten vessels including three in May 1799 which grossed £16,000. Warehouses along the Liverpool waterfront and that of Halifax where much of it was eventually sold were full of cocoa, oil, wine, brandy, dry goods, molasses, sugar and all the other commodities common in the West Indies trade.

One of the *Wentworth's* prizes, the Spanish *Seignora del Carmen* of 194 tons was converted into a privateer by her new owners. Armed to the gunwales with twenty guns, twenty barrels of powder, thirty-eight rounds of grape shot, one hundred cutlasses and a crew of ninety-six men and boys, she too made her way southward. Renamed the *Duke of Kent* in honour of the Commander-in-Chief at Halifax, she met with several successes. On one occasion she towed the prize *Santo Christo del Graz* from Puerto Rico to Liverpool despite the fact that all her masts and spars were sprung. Her cargo valued at £4,000 to £5,000, she herself was sold for a mere £88.

In October 1799, Perkins and his partners outfitted the *Lady Hammond,* a Danish prize to the *Duke of Kent.* Renamed the *Lord Spencer* after the First Lord of the Admiralty, she foundered on a reef off Cape Codero on her first voyage during which she sailed in company with the *Duke of Kent* and *Charles Mary Wentworth.* Had Captain Barss and his crew not happened to come upon the *Wentworth* they would have had to row home in the *Spencer's* tender. Instead they came to Nova Scotia courtesy of the Shelburne privateer *Nelson.*

In addition to these privateers, the Liverpool merchants with whom Perkins allied himself also held shares in the privateers *Fly, Nymph,* and *Rover.* Despite a £1,600 outfit, the *Nymph* only returned prizes valuing £1,500. There was little profit in that type of venture and the partners were likely somewhat relieved when word arrived in the fall of 1801 that the Peace of Amiens had ended the war. Almost immediately the *Rover, Duke of Kent,* and *Nymph* were sold and traded their cannons for more peaceful cargoes which, too, were West Indies bound.

Despite the brief period of peace, war broke out again in May 1803. This time Napoleon was leading France and war was to drag on until 1815 and eventually lead to war between Britain and the United States. The *Rover* was purchased by Perkins and his fellow merchants, refitted at a cost of £1,700

43

and sent out on a cruise. Captain Ben Collins behaved in a most unsatisfactory manner and the owners found themselves losing considerably more than they had spent.

During the war over two dozen Nova Scotia privateers cruised southward in search of glory and prize money. Of these, seven hailed from Liverpool, Six of which had Simeon Perkins as a shareholder. Despite the excitement which such ventures must have created, little money was made. In an entry in his famous diary in 1802 Simeon spoke of his business interests of the time and life in general. It certainly does not suggest that privateering was a very adequate manner to gain quick riches.

Tuesday, May 4th—This day, forty years ago, I arrived in this Harbour, and Spent the Greatest part of that time here. I opened a Store and Carried on the Fishery directly on my Arrival . . . in which time I have been married, & have Two Sons & Six Daughters. Have gone thro Much fatigue & Anxiety in Business, and have met with many Losses & Misfortunes, and have not added So much to my property as might be expected from the Business I have done. But have in the Main had Tolerable Health, myself & Family, for Which I have abundant reason to be thankful.

SOME FUNDY CAPTAINS

In 1809 the United States of America did something nice for the Loyalist City of Saint John. They passed a law which forbade any American citizen to trade with Great Britain or her colonies. As if that was not good enough news, the countries around the Baltic Sea were forced by the Emperor of France, none other than Napoleon himself, to refuse Great Britain badly needed naval supplies, especially timber for masts and spars. Almost immediately, angry New Englanders began smuggling goods out of the United States to the nearby ports of St. Andrews and Saint John and trading them for British goods which were in turn smuggled back into their own country. At the same time, a booming timber industry sprang up on the St. John River and its tributaries, an industry which was intended to fit the ships of the Royal Navy with New Brunswick masts and spars in place of those from the Baltic.

Saint John became the centre for both these activities, not only for New Brunswick but for the Bay of Fundy shore of Nova Scotia as well. Daily, vessels of all sizes flying both the British and American flags passed Partridge Island and made for the harbour of Saint John. Not only were American and English goods brought into port, so too were the products of the West Indies and Europe.

This well-placed natural harbour, embraced by the hilly city and its suburbs, had become a thriving marketplace. Under the protecting guns of Fort Howe at the harbour's head, wharves, warehouses, docks, timber-ponds, booms and shipyards flourished. The merchants who met daily to discuss their business affairs in the local coffee houses were brimming with satisfaction and faith in the future.

When war with the United States broke out in 1812, things got even better. Not only did the navy need even more timber, New Englanders began to smuggle more than ever before. As the naval blockade of American ports like Boston began to destroy Yankee business, the situation for Saint John improved even further. Vessels from Maine to Connecticut applied to the British for trading licences to come to British ports under British protection where they could trade their cargoes.

Wartime economic activities were not restricted to trading however. New Brunswickers along the Fundy shore had become experienced seamen and many of them began to look to privateering as a way to fatten their purses as well as protect their trading vessels from attacks by Yankee privateers. The provincial government outfitted the *Brunswicker* in the autumn of 1812 and sent her off to the Fundy mouth and Gulf of Maine where she met with success. She herself was the former American revenue cutter *Commodore Barry* which had been captured by the Royal Navy and brought into Saint John.

Not to be outdone, George Raymond and several of his business associates applied to the government in Fredericton for a letter-of-marque and outfitted the *General Smythe,* appropriately named after the province's lieutenant governor. Beginning her cruises in October 1813, she captured several American vessels including the *Penelope* valued at £7,119 and *Reward* valued at £5,232. Her young master, George Rideout, undoubtedly put his prize money to good use in providing for his recent bride Frances whom he had married in March 1813.

Despite these successes, privateering was not popular with certain powerful figures in New Brunswick and London. In their eagerness to win prizes, the cruisers often captured American vessels which were heading for British ports with their cargoes of goods smuggled out of the United States. The result was that the provincial government ceased issuing letters-of-marque.

New Brunswickers were accustomed to finding loop-holes in the law and privateering proved no exception. Many merchants and captains decided that if they could not get a licence from New Brunswick, they would simply get one in Nova Scotia. It was under these circumstances that the firm of Hugh Johnson and Son entered into partnership with Thomas Milledge and outfitted the ship *Herald*. Under Charles Simonds, whose father had come to Saint John in the 1760's, she sallied forth into the Fundy tides. With 10 guns and 25 men she captured five schooners and a sloop in a matter of months. In his later years, Simonds entered politics and became Speaker of the House of Assembly in Fredericton.

A few weeks after the *Herald* acquired her letter-of-marque, Noah Disbrow, John Clark and Hugh Doyle sent the schooner *Hare* after American shipping. James Reid soon gave them a return on their investment for he brought in the sloop *Hero* and brig *Recovery*. A short time later he left the *Hare* to his first lieutenant James Godsoe and took command of the privateer *Snap Dragon*.

47

Saint John attracted Nova Scotians as well. John Harris came from Annapolis to command the sloop *Dart* which had great successes against the Americans. Capturing several schooners, he fattened his purse with the addition of two full-rigged ships, the *Cuba* and *Union*. Her first cruise in 1813 provided some £500 prize money for each crew member. Like so many privateers, the *Dart* ventured out once too often. Off Point Judith, Maine, she was attacked by an American revenue cutter and captured. Her ship's log is located in the Archives of the New Brunswick Museum.

Undoubtedly the most famous of the Saint John privateersmen was Caleb Seely. Tall and handsome at 26 years of age, he left the West Indies trade and took command of the privateer *Star* in 1813. Despite his youth, he quickly returned to port with three prizes, the sloops *Elizabeth* and *Resolution* and the pinky *Flower*. Caleb was ambitious, too, a quality which may have been the basis of a friendship which was to change his life considerably.

48

Privateer schooner "Liverpool Packet", 1811-1815 from a painting by Thomas Hayhurst. Reproduced with permission of Bowater Mersey Paper Company.

Sometime before 1813 he had met an equally ambitious Nova Scotian, Enos Collins, who had spent his early life in Liverpool. Enos had been involved in the West Indies trade as well as in privateering exploits in the Caribbean and it may have been there that they first met. Through the years Enos had outgrown the limited commercial life of Liverpool and had moved his growing business to Halifax. When the War of 1812 broke out he had invested wisely in the privateer *Liverpool Packet* and had received a large enough return on his investment that her loss in June 1813 had been little more than a nuisance.

When the *Liverpool Packet* was recaptured off Mount Desert, she was taken into Saint John. It may have been at this time that Caleb decided to move up in the world and seek command of her, for soon after she was purchased by the Halifax firm of Collins and Allison on November 9, 1813, Seeley was named commander. He sold his business interests in Saint John and moved to the heart of the privateering trade, Liverpool.

The *Packet's* new letter of-marque was issued by Sir John Sherbrooke in Halifax on November 25, 1813, and Caleb remained her master for the next eleven months. During that time he ranged the American coast from Maine to the approaches of New York Harbour and brought some fourteen prizes before the Court of Vice-Admiralty for condemnation. In one four-day period he is reputed to have captured prizes valuing more than $100,000.

While Caleb was ambitious, he was not careless. In October 1814 he passed his command on to Benjamin Knaut of Liverpool and devoted his energies to building a successful shipping business of his own. Interestingly enough, he married Phoebe Collins, Eno's sister and in 1816 purchased Simeon Perkins' house from Perkins' widow. He must have maintained a fairly close connection with his old home for his third wife, Jane Sancton, was a Saint John girl. Caleb died in Liverpool on Valentine's Day 1869 at the age of eighty-one, having led a successful business life. He did not, however, achieve the heights of his brother-in-law Enos who died a few years later as one of the wealthiest men in North America. It is interesting that a small portion of his wealth came to him through his interest in privateers.

It may at first seem strange to have a book on privateering include a section on an infantry regiment. It may seem even stranger when the membership of the regiment was drawn almost entirely from farmers and country gentlemen. It may seem stranger still that the men and women of the King's Orange Rangers were not Nova Scotians, but were largely from New York and New Jersey. Why then, would they have a place here. This in brief, is their story.

William Bayard of Greenwich Village, New York, was determined to support the Crown in the civil war we now call the American Revolution. He did in December 1776 by forming the King's Orange Rangers. Established as a Royal Provincial Regiment its officers and men came~ largely from New York and New Jersey. The name "Orange" came from Orange County, New York where Bayard had large land holdings.

The King's Orange Rangers saw action in New York and New Jersey. The were present at actions at Kingsbridge, Haarlam Heights and the capture of Fort Knyphausen. They also carried out raids against rebels in coastal New Jersey in the vicinity of Hobookan. The regiment gained an unfortunate reputation for poor discipline, interminable fractiousness particularly among its officers and for desertion. In part this probably can be attributed to the fact that Bayard chose his son John as commanding officer and at the very least, his age and personality, appear to have made him unfit for the challenge of command.

The rumour that they were being sent to Nova Scotia so enraged the soldiers that they had to be confined on board the transport ship days in advance of setting sail. To further allay their fears, they were told they were being sent to the south. In November 1778 however, the King's Orange Rangers were transported to Halifax where they were to form part of the colony's garrison. Their duties included protection of the Eastern Battery (later Fort Cumberland) and from time to time quelling rebel spirits in the Annapolis Valley, especially around Cornwallis Township. In 1782 after the capture and pillage of Lunenburg, Captain Bethel's Company was sent there to protect the community from further depredation.

The township which suffered most as a consequence of rebel American activity was Liverpool. What particularly galled the citizens was that most of the privateers like themselves, were from Massachusetts. In response to continued entreaties for protection from community leaders, the government in Halifax sent Captain Howard's Company of the King's Orange Rangers as a garrison to protect the South Shore seaport.

Initially the King's Orange Rangers were billeted in the town. This proved as disastrous in Liverpool as it had in New England for the locals and the soldiers simply did not mix. Consequently the soldiers and their officers moved well outside town to the vicinity of Fort Point. The recently built Freeman house barracked a number of the soldiers while the officers found rooms in Dexter's Tavern. Later a number of the enlisted men who had brought their families with them built homes of sods to protect them from the inclement Nova Scotia winter.

Capt. John Howard was intent on putting his detachment to good use. He undoubtedly realized that it was far better for the men under his command to be taking the offensive wherever possible. In early June 1779, Howard proposed going out in a vessel with his soldiers to try to capture a privateer which had been reported in the Liverpool area. Capt. Bradford agreed to take his schooner and serve as sailing master. In addition to the crew, some forty of the King's Orange Rangers embarked for the chase. On the 4th, the schooner got out of the harbour slowly, but was rewarded by soon seeing another which was believed to be the rebel privateer. By the morning of the 5th rumours were flying around Liverpool that there had been an engagement between the KOR and the rebel. Around 10 AM the Rangers' schooner beat up the harbour. They had attacked the rebel schooner, captured its boat and lieutenant and two men and killed a number of rebels. The prisoners including the lieutenant and brothers Thomas and George Thomas were given their parole o~ promise that they would not leave town and would report every twenty-four hours.

On October 2nd, Capt. Cobb and Peter Collins made their way into Liverpool having come from Port Medway. They reported that a Congress privateer came into the harbour and seized their vessels and took them out to sea. Cobb's in fact belonged to Joseph Tinkham. Elkanah Freeman was taken away in the Tinkham schooner and Thomas Cook in Collins' smaller schooner. In likelihood they would serve as "davvy men" when the vessels were condemned as prizes of war.

On the 3rd, Capt. Howard with a party of King's Orange Rangers joined Tinkham, Collins and others in three boats in order to try to retake the lost Liverpool vessels. They returned that evening not having found any sign of them. Later in the day Snow Parker arrived in Liverpool and related that both James Knowles and Joseph Verge were captured near Green Island. The cargo included King's provisions and "Considerable Goods for Hallet Collins, & James McDonald, & Rum for Capt. Wm. Freeman.
The next day Snow Parker's shallop was fitted out to go in search of Knowles. Several of the town's prominent citizens went in her. Capt. Howard also fitted out John Hopkins' shallop and manned it with Lieutenant McLeod and Lieutenant Stewart as well as several King's Orange Rangers. They returned the following day without success. This pattern continued through the autumn when Howard with 20 King's Orange Rangers and 10 of the Queens County Militia and others went to Port Medway in order to try to capture another privateer.

The most significant result of these events lay in the decision born of frustration with losses by the citizens' own countrymen. On October 6th Perkins writes, "We meet again to conclude about a Privateer, & agree so far as to raise £300, & Petition Government to Lend us some Guns, & Provide us with Ammunition." On November 29th a meeting was held at Mrs. Snows to discuss further the arming of a Liverpool vessel as a privateer. Those attending included Perkins, Capt. Collins, Capt. Howard, Mr. Tinkham, Captain William Freeman, Captain Bartlett Bradford, Mr. McDonald and Captain John Howard. They agreed to outfit the schooner *Lucy* as the first of the Liverpool privateers. On

December 8th a further meeting was held at Mrs. Snow's respecting the privateer *Lucy* which again included Captain Howard. A number of candidates were considered as captain, the final choice falling on Bartlett Bradford. On the 13th it was settled that there would be 14 shareholders in the *Lucy* including Capt. Howard with two shares.

February 5th 1780 the *Lucy* arrived in Liverpool with two prizes. They were the sloop *Sally,* Benjamin Cole, Master and the schooner *Little Joe,* Giles Latham, Master. Upon examining Cole's mate, a Mr. Brown, it is discovered that he was bound for the states which makes her a legitimate prize. The next day all parties appear before Samuel Hunt in order for testimony to be heard regarding the captured vessels. Cole has several of his crew appear on his behalf supporting his statement that he was on legitimate business and was not providing assistance to the rebels. Cole's mate tells a very different story. The prizes were sent to Halifax and condemned by the Court of Vice-Admiralty, notification reaching Liverpool on March 18th.

Throughout the winter months the King's Orange Rangers continued to provide security along the Queens County coast frequenting both Port Medway and Port Mouton. In early march Howard and party of soldiers went to the westward with a warrant from Perkins to "Defend & Swear the Inhabitants". Capt. Howard took the opportunity to invest further in the *Lucy* She was sold at auction in Liverpool for £395 on March 21st, but continued her life as a privateer with a different mix of owners. On the 26th *Lucy* sailed for Halifax with Capt. Howard on board.

On June 7th the *Lucy* went over the bar at the mouth of the Mersey and anchored off Fort Point. At dinner time it was reported that two schooners, possibly privateers, had gone in behind Coffins Island. Lt. Stewart and a dozen KORs went out in her, but found no enemy vessels. On the 24th Perkins dined with the officers of the KOR in "their Tower in Mr. Cameron's Garden"

On June 27th, Snow Parker arrived with a prize which had been taken by the *Lucy*. She was a Schooner of about 40 tonnes "on the New Model and sails very fast". She had been launched only two weeks before and hailed from Plymouth. Three other prizes were captured by the *Lucy* on the same cruise. The arrival of the prize proved timely. John Doggett came to town from Port Mouton saying that a privateer shallop had taken his shallop as well as Mr. Arnold's and also a vessel belonging to a man from Argyle. The prize was quickly readied for sea and Captain Howard put 25 KORs under command of Lieutenant Mcleod on board. Snow Parker, four other privateersmen, Perkins' son Roger and Edward Howard also went on board.

Next day the armed schooner returned with the *Lucy's* prize retaken. Four of the recaptured prize's crew were soldiers of Captain Solomon's company of marines. The prisoners were put ashore and the militia ordered to place them under guard. Meanwhile, the armed schooner returned to sea with 20 KOR under Lt. McLeod.

Early on the morning of July 30th word reached Perkins that the *Delight* which had been lying at Perkins' wharf, had been taken through the night. captain Joseph Barss's privateer *Dispatch* was sent in pursuit with Captain Howard putting 20 of the KORs on board. The only immediate result was the discovery of Harrington's shallop which was disabled. A skiff belonging to the *Lucy* came in and reported that the culprit was Captain Cole whose own vessel the Sally had been taken by *Lucy* earlier in the year. Cole's privateer was said to be armed with 5 iron and 5 wooden guns. The Lucy was made ready for sea and Captain Howard and 20 KORs went on board with eh intention of hunting Cole down, but no one would go as crew.

September 13th, 1780 was the day the Yankee privateers came to town with the intention of laying it waste. Shortly after midnight Captain Benjamin Cole in his privateer *Surprise* and with the consort *Delight* which had only a short while before be taken from Liverpool, slipped into Ballast Cove and sent most of their 70 men ashore. By 4:00AM they had overpowered the sentries and were in possession of Fort Point."At Four O'Clock in the morning, three of the Officers, all the Soldiers but Six, the Fort & Ammunition, the Gunner, and Some of the Inhabitants, with a Number of the Militia Arms, were in Possession of Capt, Cole" wrote Perkins. Captain Howard, the other captured KOR officers and Sheriff Joseph Tinkham who had also been captured, were taken to Cole's schooner and place under guard.

Perkins was awakened at about 3:00 AM by Prince Snow and advised that the fort had been captured along with most of the officers and that the towns people living at the Point were also captive. Lieutenant McLeod and Ensign Cameron soon appeared at Perkins house and confirmed the alarming state of affairs. One of the KOR had deserted to the privateers and spread the rumor among the townsfolk that the enemy numbered 500 or more, that there were several ships in the harbour and that all the KOR had joined them.

Perkins dispatched his son Roger to town to raise the alarm and to get Captain West and Captain Freeman and all others he could and get them under arms. Roger returned in short measure to report that the people were disheartened and were not inclined to make any resistance and they believed their situation to be desperate. They believed the best thing to do was simply be quiet.

Prince Snow, Roger Perkins and Ensign Cameron were active in reconnoitering and as dawn approached, they assured Perkins that there were in fact only two schooners in the harbour. Perkins rightly conjectured that this meant the real number of privateers on shore at the Fort was more likely in the range of 40-50. He also concluded that the commander wa Captain Cole who had been seen so frequently in the area in recent weeks.

After disarming the soldiers and the inhabitants at the Fort, Cole began to move up the road from the Fort which lead past Perkins house to the town. On the way he encountered Perkins man John Heater whom he disarmed and took prisoner. Cole was furious with Captain Bartlett Bradford who as captain of the Liverpool privateer *Lucy* had captured Cole's schooner *Sally* eight months before.

Meanwhile, Perkins was advised by Benajah Collins, Hal let Collins and Captain Ross to try to take Cole prisoner before he got to the town. By this time the town people were beginning to take some courage and show indications of the will to fight the invaders.

Consequently, Perkins ordered Ensign Cameron, Prince Snow, Roger Perkins, John Campbell and John Lewin Jr. to proceed down the road to the Fort and to apprehend Cole and his men. They lay in wait for them at Snow Parker's gate, surprised and disarmed them in short order. Captain Ross took Cole as his prisoner and marched him off to be interrogated by Perkins. More of Cole's men came up the road as far as the Widow (Abigail) Collins (wife of Joseph Collins who had died January 12, 1772). There they saw a number of Perkins men, opened fire on them and beat a hasty retreat towards the Fort.

Captain Ross took Cole to Perkins house where he was asked by the colonel if he had any terms to propose respecting an accommodation. Perkins now dispatched Benajah Collins to the Fort with a letter from Cole advising his men that he was a prisoner and to propose that a one hour cease fire be observed while terms of accommodation were worked out. Captain Lane who was in charge of the Fort sent a man under a flag of truce to determine if in fact the letter Collins carried was in Cole's handwriting. This confirmed, negotiations were opened.

Cole opened the negotiations saying that if Lane was in agreement, he would leave Liverpool if he was given the King's stores and was paid for the loss of the *Sally*. Perkins, knowing that Cole's bargaining power was pretty slim countered. He offered that Captain Howard, Lieutenant McLeod and Lieutenant Stewart should be exchanged for Captain Cole, that there should be mutual exchange of all prisoners, all property should be restored and the King's stores left in tact. Further, Perkins offered to give the privateers 24 hours to get away from Liverpool before any chase was given. Additionally, by now the townspeople had found their backbone and Cole was advised that the militia was armed and prepared for a fight. Cole agreed and a letter was sent to Captain Lane outlining the proposal.

Lane returned with the flag of truce and tried to present an alternate proposal, but to no avail. As Perkins wrote in his diary, "he endeavoured to persuade me to other terms, but to no purpose. I found by this time that the militia were many of them under Arms & Determined to fight, & even to Storm the Fort, if Necessary." Lane finally complied and he and Captain Joseph Freeman departed for the Fort with the article of convention as agreed upon. The captured KORs were released and Captain Howard, the other captured officers of the KOR and Joseph Tinkham were brought on shore from Cole's schooner.

Captain Lane evacuated the Fort and the Militia marched in. In a final negotiation, Cole and Lane agreed to a 25 guinea ransom for Captain Dean's brig which they had captured during the night.

The privateers got under way and beat out the harbour. When they reached about Moose Harbour, a small Halifax privateer commanded by Captain Hill and armed with three carriage guns and a swivel hove in sight. Immediately the Americans broke their agreement and commenced firing on the smaller vessel. In return, the guns at the Fort were loaded and fired towards the enemy privateers although they were too far off to do any damage. The plucky Halifax privateer stood the enemy fire. The Americans came along side her and called for boarding, but it never happened. They broke off the action heading to the eastward and leaving one of Hill's crew dead and two wounded. A few days later it was confirmed that after the action Cole and Lane had limped into Port Medway to lick his wounds. Hill had bested him for the Americans had three killed and two wounded. Both Captain Dean's brig and the Halifax privateer came into the river for greater safety.

Over the next few days Liverpool's community leaders met to discuss how they could better protect themselves against marauders like Cole. On the 15th they convened at the Fort where they concluded that at the very least they should build a picket fence and perhaps build a block house and a barrack within the pickets. They agree that the £50 granted by the Assembly for the Militia should be put towards a block house.

The King's Orange Rangers remained in Liverpool until August 1783. Setting aside their dark moment of September 13th, 1780 they had provided defence against the rebels and had acted as leaders in serving as surrogate marines on board various local vessels. they had successfully attacked rebel privateers and had drawn blood. Their captain had invested in the initial two cruises of the first Liverpool privateer *Lucy*. All in all, they made a positive contribution to the development of Liverpool as the *Port of the Privateers*.

EPILOGUE

This little book was first published 21 years ago and in the interviewing years it has sold several thousand copies, Originally published by Bill McCurdy's Petheric Press, this new edition has been made possible by the Region of Queens Municipality which has underwritten printing costs. All profits from the sale of the book are donated by the author equally between Fort Point Lighthouse Museum and the Queens historical re-enactment society, King's Orange Rangers. This is fitting as both Fort Point and the King's Orange Rangers are part of our privateering heritage.

So here it is, the phenomenon of privateering in a nutshell. It was not comparable to piracy although a few overzealous privateersmen came awfully close to crossing the line separating them. Similarly, it was not conducted by ruthless adventurer nor by dashing naval heroes, but rather by seamen and ships' masters who would far sooner have been following more peaceful pursuits. None made a fortune from privateering although a few businessmen were able to sustain some considerable financial gain. Finally, the law of the sea rather than being abused was given more careful prominence through privateering for, in the best tradition of British justice, the onus lay on the captor to prove the "guilt" of the vessel and cargo brought to court. In fact, it was respectable occupation carried on by respectable men, men who had long before learned to adapt themselves to conditions which the sea and their governments imposed upon them.

GLOSSARY

ALOFT — High above the deck of a ship

BALLAST — A heavy material carried in a vessel to give it stability (re: rocks off a beach)

BALTIMORE CLIPPER — A swift schooner rigged vessel with a particularly sharp bow

BARQUE — Three masted vessel with fore and mainmasts square rigged. The mizzen carried on a square rig aloft with a spanker below

BARQUENTINE — Three masted vessel with foremast square-rigged, the main and mizzen carrying gaff rigs

BEAT TO QUARTERS — Calling of a crew, usually by the beat of a drum, to their battle stations

BEND — Fastening a sail to a yard

BLUENOSE — A Nova Scotian

BOATSWAIN (BOSUN) — Petty officer in charge of the deck crew

BOW — Front end of a vessel

BOWER ANCHOR — Bow anchor

BRIG — Fairly small vessel two masted vessel with the foremast squire-rigged, the mainmast carrying a gaff mainsail

BRIGANTINE — Fairly small vessel with two square- rigged masts

BURTHERN — Weight

CANVAS — Material of varying weights used in sails

CLOSE TO THE WIND — Sailing a vessel so that the bow points as closely in the direction of the wind as possible without affecting the forward motion of the vessel

63

COHORN — Type of cannon

CRANK — Term applied to a vessel which does not handle well

DOCKYARD — A place with docks, machinery and supplies for repairing or building ships

DRAUGHT — Depth of a vessel from waterline to keel

FATHOM — Depth of six feet

FETTERS — Chains used for imprisoning a person, handcuffs

GLASS — A timer like an eggtimer used to keep time on shipboard. It took one-half hour for the sand to run from top to bottom

GRAPPLING IRON — Anchor like implement thrown from one vessel to another in order to fasten them together

HANDS — Ordinary seamen

HOLD — Part of a vessel where the cargo is carried

HOVE — Old past tense for heave

HULK — The hull of an old dismantled ship

LEAD — A weight for sounding depths at sea

LEE — Side opposite the wind

MANIFEST — Itemized list of a ship's cargo

RUN — Sail rapidly, usually with the wind directly astern

SCHOONER — Usually a two masted vessel with triangular gaff-rigged sails

SHORTEN SAIL — To remove sails in order to cut down the influence of the wind on a vessel

SLOOP — Single masted sailing vessel, usually small

SPANISH MAIN — Old name for the coast of modern Venezuela

SPAR — Mast of a vessel or the yards to which the sails are fastened or bent

SQUALL — Brief violent storm, usually with snow or rain

STEP — To set a mast in the base upon which it stands

STERN — Back end of a vessel

SWAB — Long-handled brush for cleaning the barrel of a gun

SWIVEL — A gun mounted in such a way that it can be turned horizontally or vertically for aiming

WADDING — Soft material packed into a gun muzzle as part of the charge

WARP — A rope used to move a vessel into position

WEAR — To turn a ship by swinging its bow away from the wind

WINDWARD — The side facing the wind

BIBLIOGRAPHY

1 Blakeley, Phyllis R., "An Adventure with a Privateer", **Nova Scotia Historical Quarterly** vol. 2, No. 2, 1972. pp. 163-172.

2 Blakeley, Phyllis R., **Nova Scotia,** Toronto, Dent, 1972

3 Douglas, W. A. B, "The Sea Militia of Nova Scotia 1749-1755: A Comment on Naval Poilcy," **Canadian Historical Review.** vol. xlvii, No. 1, 1966. pp. 22-37

4 Hamilton William B., **Local History in Atlantic Canada,** Toronto. Macmillan, 1974

5 Leefe, John, "A Bluenose Privateer of 1812," **Nova Scotia Historical Quarterly,** vol. 3, No. 1, 1973. pp. 1-20

6 Leefe, John, "The Bounty Hunter," **Nova Scotia Historical Quarterly,** vol. 3, No. 4, 1973. pp. 333-340

7 MacBeath, George, **New Brunswick,** Toronto. Gage, 1965

8 MacMechan, Archibald, **Old Province Tales,** Toronto, McClelland and Stewart, 1924. pp. 163-182

9 More, James F., **The History of Queens County N.S.,** Belleville, Mika Studio, 1972

10 Millane, George, "The Privateers of Nova Scotia; 1756-1783," **Colections of the Nova Scotia Historical Society,** vol. xx

11 Nichols, G. E. E., "Nova Scotia Privateers", **Collections of the Nova Scotia Historical Society,** vol. xiii

12 Raddall, Thomas H., **Pride's Fancy,** Toronto, McClelland and Stewart. 1973

13 Raddall, Thomas H., **The Rover,** Toronto, Macmillan, 1958

14 Snider, C. H. J., **In the Wake of the Eighteen Twelvers,** Toronto, McClelland and Stewart

15 Snider, C. H. J., **Under the Red Jack,** Toronto, McLellan and Stewart.

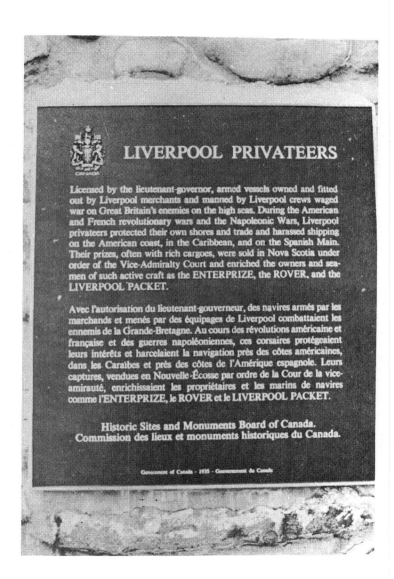

LIVERPOOL PRIVATEERS

Licensed by the lieutenant-governor, armed vessels owned and fitted out by Liverpool merchants and manned by Liverpool crews waged war on Great Britain's enemies on the high seas. During the American and French revolutionary wars and the Napoleonic Wars, Liverpool privateers protected their own shores and trade and harassed shipping on the American coast, in the Caribbean, and on the Spanish Main. Their prizes, often with rich cargoes, were sold in Nova Scotia under order of the Vice-Admiralty Court and enriched the owners and seamen of such active craft as the ENTERPRIZE, the ROVER, and the LIVERPOOL PACKET.

Avec l'autorisation du lieutenant-gouverneur, des navires armés par les marchands et menés par des équipages de Liverpool combattaient les ennemis de la Grande-Bretagne. Au cours des révolutions américaine et française et des guerres napoléoniennes, ces corsaires protégeaient leurs intérêts et harcelaient la navigation près des côtes américaines, dans les Caraïbes et près des côtes de l'Amérique espagnole. Leurs captures, vendues en Nouvelle-Écosse par ordre de la Cour de la vice-amirauté, enrichissaient les propriétaires et les marins de navires comme l'ENTERPRIZE, le ROVER et le LIVERPOOL PACKET.

Historic Sites and Monuments Board of Canada.
Commission des lieux et monuments historiques du Canada.

Government of Canada - 1935 - Gouvernement du Canada

Bronze plaque on the stone Cairn at Fort Point, Liverpool.